CHISELED TEETH

Ashley Logan

ISBN: 9798443683157

Cerasus Poetry
London N22 6LY

cerasuspoetry.com

for all who need to remember there is still time to bloom

CONTENTS

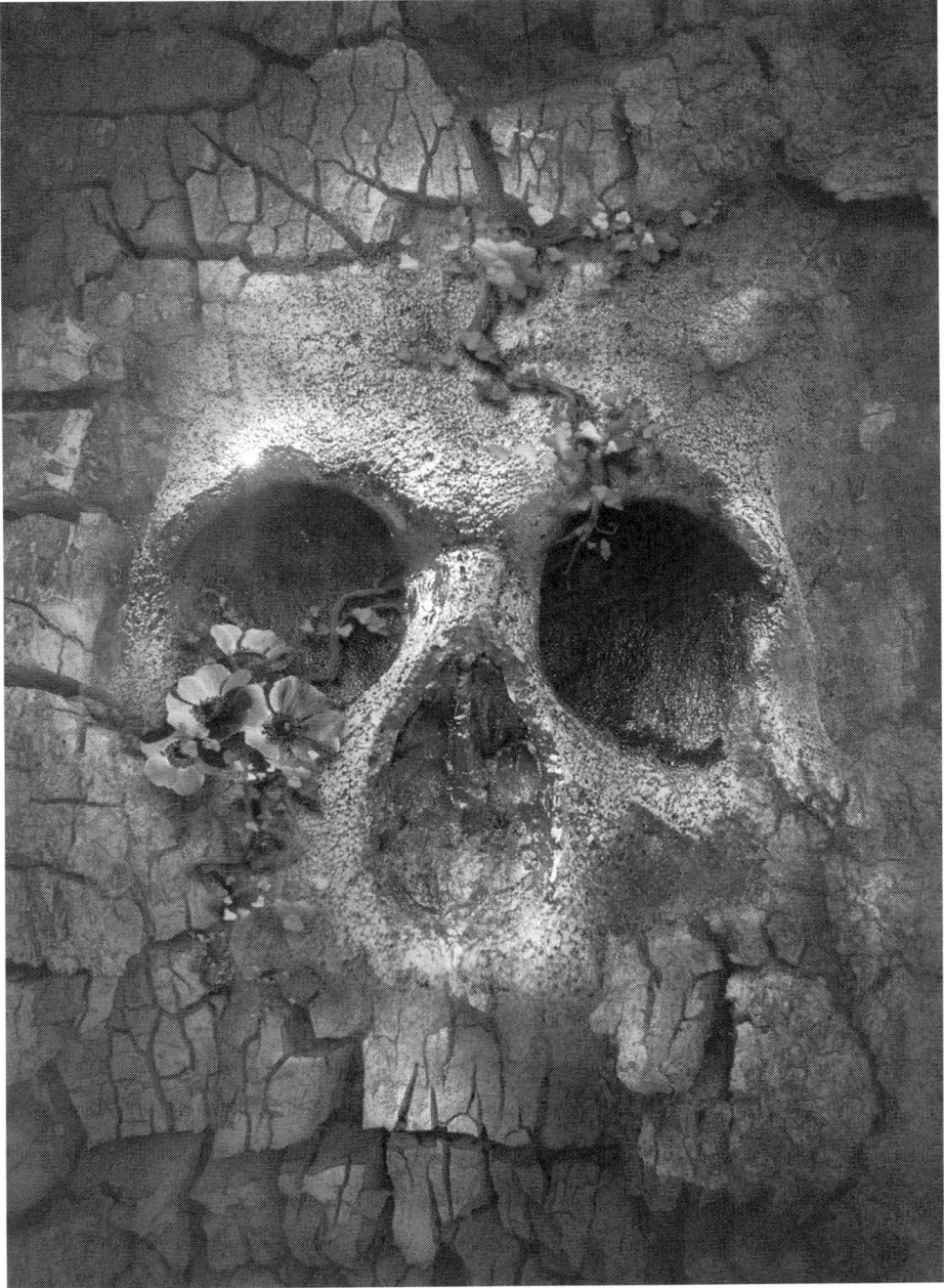

Don't Pick The Flowers

He told her once
that he preferred the wildflowers,
the evening primrose and the silver aster,
to the more famous blooms.

Wild though they were,
their names conjured between his lips,
names he whispered in her ear:
a secret only they were strong enough to know.

She allowed the wild to blossom in the back of her jaw,
chiseled teeth clenched and feral.
They tread across the meadow.

He dared not pick a tiny bluet for her.
She hated their little deaths.
Instead he held out his hand,
and she could feel nature's grasp.

Consequences

Beneath my right shoulder
blade is a wound. It pains me
from time to time, cause unknown,
a fierce reminder that my body
still has secrets. It does not bleed,
this wound. Sometimes what hurts
is not wrong after all. We adapt.
I think about my mother who
does not sleep, who shuffles in the dark.
She would say it is without purpose.
With wilted wrists, my hands hover,
and search. Sometimes what is wrong
does not hurt. My family is made
of the untold, and I am no different.
There is a language for it, home.

Gossip

Your open mouth
is a parenthesis,
every word
an afterthought
that should have
been swallowed,
contained
at the lips,
but you seem to enjoy
the slough
from your tongue,
dead words scraped
from the tissue
and caught
in the teeth.
The bored
have no memory
of the things
they have said,
trouble for you,
unhinging your jaw
to reveal
sentences
formed
from such eagerness
to impress.

The tiny comma
in the back
of your throat
attempts to pause —
but you can't help
yourself; the silence
torments you,
so you beg
for audience.
You're spliced
and hold
no thing sacred,
nothing secret.
Your mouth is
a leaking wound,
a parenthetical mistake,
every word unsought
and then forgotten
at the lips,
those brackets
that will one day
find each other —
or so I hope
(for you).

What Does Safety Mean and What Does It Cost?

I carry an umbrella even with no chance for rain.
It cost me two dollars when I bought it,
though I don't remember where.

I do remember I wore a yellow sweater,
wrapped around my body tight in a hug.
I held the umbrella aloft, a shield from the sun

that was bright but cold. The sweater I bought at a thrift store,
also for two dollars, and though it was worn, it remained
bright and warm. I found safety for the price of four dollars,

the cost of which I felt I could not afford at the time.
And yet. Shelter and security came from eight quarters
and twenty dimes, a weight once carried in tiny pockets

of too-small jeans. Emptied now, I bring my umbrella
in case of. In case of everything. I once took a walk and
discovered yellow daffodils that I could clutch in one hand,

umbrella in the other, and together we cocooned
beneath my two dollar roof. I then left my sweater
on a bench to pass along a note of hope.

Sometimes when I spot a fleck of yellow wander the streets,
I wonder if their pockets are as light as mine. I wonder if they,
too, carry protection everywhere, and if so, what did it cost?

A Letter To My Father

If I could, I'd stoke your fire,
but you would insist I place my body on the flames,
a serving of respect that is curated by your righteousness.
I can name every line in my palm, hands that
have aged in conjunction with your anger.
Your God seems to speak through your mouth,
and yet I open mine and receive silence.
An ache builds beneath my jaw and
bleeds onto my tongue and coats my teeth,
a gruesome grin that I keep. I also keep
fireflies in my pockets, remembrances of a time
when I could not imagine you as anything
but a father. I am not so young now, and if
you've taught me anything, it is that forgiveness
does not come cheap if at all. Does your God know?
I often think about another version of me,
the version that pleases you and is somehow the daughter
neither my sister nor I have managed to be.
This version perhaps names her children after Orion
and stands in your backyard with the new waterfall,
the one your wife insisted upon, and perhaps I take
a drag as you take a swig as conversation wafts
over the grill about your life and theirs. Maybe they
would even know one another, a bonfire built
to warm rather than destroy and captured in the
reflections of their eyes, orbs that speak
to a simpler relationship, one not strife with danger.
Perhaps in this scenario you would never say you
should have been able to choose the child you wanted.
Perhaps in this scenario I could be that child.

Electroconvulsive Therapy Made Me Forget Many Things But Not Grief

It is quiet when you forget.
At first.
They warn you that the stimulation will result
in memory loss, but they don't tell you that
what you'll be left with is grief.
You will trade your recollection for your mind.
You will face a gaping hole where experience used to be.
There is sadness in forgetfulness, but you'll regain yourself, too.
Pain fades and scars emerge.
It is slow but not gentle –
unfortunately.
There is a price for everything. This, too.
That is why there is grief – you are better
and yet
you cannot remember how or why.
It is quiet when you forget because
the silence is what remains.
After.
The silence is a sorrow sonnet, a reminder of not what was lost
but instead of the fact that you lost it.
Say hello, though, now.
Introductions are my new saviors,
tiny initiations of person, place, and thing.
Petrified and preserved,
I am returned.
It is not so quiet.

To The Ruins of Me

I am told you cannot run from yourself,
a truth that became stuck between
my teeth, wedged and chewed the
more I spoke, ate, breathed.

I escaped to the Alps of Germany
in order to feel small, but instead
I was transformed by the rock, a
quiet story of becoming. I spelled
my name in the cracks, discovered
eternity with my hands, my tongue.
How large I feel. How small I am.

Romania's countryside sang
a hymn that I could believe,
and I balanced my mind in
the still waters of Venice.

The stray cats in Rome came free
to my hands. They rubbed their
little bodies against my palms,
and I thought about worth,
how much of it I could stand.

I pick at my teeth now with my tongue.
I feel how hard the truth has become.

Peak, South Carolina

I found a picture of an eyeball online
with veins that stretched and curved,
winter oaks in a forest.   How amazing

to glimpse the wild that pervades
behind our eyelids, a complicated but humble
jungle birthing what is ocular, singular.

The untamed parts of myself
are reflected in mirrors that I dare not touch
for I was taught my skin is forbidden,   even to me.

So, I seek out abandoned places   – dilapidated churches,
decrepit train depots, derelict homes –
and they remind me of my body.

We are also built to decay.

Left Again

The first thing I notice
about this old storeroom
is that it's not empty.
In the silence, its history
shouts and I feel
like joining in. It reminds
me too much of how
many times I've been
abandoned. How
there is somehow always
a dirty stuffed bear left behind
with the dingy mattresses,
misplaced papers, and
overturned chairs.
I identify as both
the leaving and the left,
the departing and
the ditched. I have
forgotten myself and yet
remember everything
else. I am not scared,
though perhaps I should
be – embarrassed and
relieved by the way
in which I love and I love.
The moon pelts the
dark with its loneliness,
and I look up through the
broken slats of the roof
to meet her gaze for I
know about the hope
that singles you
out when there is
nothing else left behind.
I take home the decay
and scatter my name,
graffiti on both the fallen
walls and my tender skin:
leave again, left again.

Trespass During The Day

We picked the fluorescent lights
off the ground, left behind with
the dank and dust. Held them
in our hands. Felt the smooth, cool bulbs
with our dirty fingers. Before us stretched
the deserted floor plan with an open ceiling
(nature found its way in before we did)
as pools of sunlight reflected broken glass
and puddles of waste and water.
We slung the bulbs over our shoulders, heard
the crunch of leaves and glass beneath our feet
as we walked the distance of the warehouse.
A game for all of our senses. Felt the slight
breeze from outside and peered into the murk.
Eyed how far we could throw. Watched.
As the bulbs took flight, long white glimmers,
the man-made stars spiraled across the dark
before they crashed to the ground. Shattered.
As though this trespass was research and
destruction was our portfolio in production.
Maybe. It was beautiful, cathartic. We never
stopped to think what that might mean.

Nature Walks Remind Me Of History

Picture it:
a camouflage moth
who rests on a concrete wall.

I ask if she feels safe.

Her brown and tan wings
a stark reply to the white
surroundings.

When is the last time

someone asked her that?
The moth twitches.
She is not where she should be,

(or) she is not blended in,

which says more about
us as neighbors than it does
about her ability to hide

in the plainest of sights.

Dreamscape

My grandmother asks how I like to take my coffee,
and I tell her just a little bit of honey is fine, please,
as we settle at the kitchen table, and she then asks
how goes my writing, and I tell her how I create
memories with her ghost as I pour from an invisible
pot to fill our cups, and this is grief, I think,
speaking through me as though my god is sorrow
and sorrow is my god, and she understands
this without my explanation, so she
pushes a pen towards me and tells me to go,
but I linger and watch for the suggestive smirk,
a comma etched into her face, forever
a formed pause in which we can meet, and
so I take my leave, and she bids me farewell,
and memory manages to find us in the abstract,
this place, doesn't it, or so I've found, but
my grandmother would know as she clears the table
and pours the coffee down the sink with a wink.

Enough

I wanted to feel alive
so I spent myself:
a commodity,
hands changed,
hands dirty,
hands unrelented.
I blame me for
where we are,
but there's still injustice
in the way you look
at me. After everything,
for all the space I give
you, less of me remains.
It's as though forgiveness
is a beast, a fanged wolf
that signals how I don't
belong: here. It has come
for me, though, welcome
home. Oh, I will run.
I've spent enough time
making myself small
so that you could
pretend I was yours.

Spider-Webs and Dishwater

Found in the dingy dishwater,
the gathered puddles on the porch,
the decay of the day continues on.
I've counted the hours with
fatigued fingers. An aberrant call
for absolution is thrown out
the cracked windows and tumbles
to the feet of passers-by who
step over, step around, step until
left behind. Cross-stitched eyes
of blue watch unblinking and hands
proffer every thing ever once held,
a shadowed gesture. Underneath
fingernails, my own skin, brought
to my lips and cleaned with my teeth:
consumed. The draw of evening pulls
me back, and I am amused. The day turns
itself over eventually. Meanwhile.
Isn't this what it is to live? I ask.
I skip out into the night, entangled
in the silvery threads of web, yes.

Bathroom Therapy

Slow things down, take the time to listen to the girl
who cries in the stall next door, recall the way your
own chest heaves in response, connected now, neighbors,
and I understand her, hear her, see her, and I tell her
the love will come, the ache will fade, the weight will lift,
just hold on, even as I also sit on toilet lids and stare
at my feet and wonder at how the stranger next door could
be so kind as to offer me a lifeline before we know one's names,
for with every word, we become infinite and larger, we become
each other's marker, and somehow there is comfort in
the unknown, and somehow there is comfort in how we listen
to these tiny stories, and somehow there is comfort in our meeting
at the mirror, where we witness our reflections, sentient echoes
that remind us to breathe and watch as we do, and this is
a lesson in how to slow things down, this is taking the time
to figure things out, this is when we note how to be human.

Little Gods

I have found little gods
in the vessels of my lungs.
How they create then push me.
There are little deities behind my eyes
that seek always for the beyond.
Perhaps I am not ruined, they find.
There is a sentence that lives within me.
We all have one, the little gods say.
Perhaps it is the moss beneath aged rocks
or the extended limbs of a longleaf pine
or maybe it is more internal,
central, you know the way home.
It is endless, the sentence, made up
by fragments that quirk with discovery.
I have always wondered what mine might be.
Whisper it now, little gods.
Call yourself by name.

I No Longer Dream At Night

Bodies shift in beds and send a signal
that restlessness comes for those who sin,
inescapable,
while chapped mouths gape,
a silent question breathed
through their lips
and in flight above
their heads,
a wanted spirit.
This is the way the night ends,
with dawn shackled to
fleshy ankles that rise, rise
in a shuffle and reach
towards bagels and coffee and eggs
while bleary-eyed and stirring.
The books on the kitchen counter
are thrillers, and pages of
dread and terror rescind the calm
the morning is supposed to bring,
but those are just stories,
unlike the horror of waking
when we haven't slept at all.
Witness the calamity of this mess,
the way bony fingers curl
around their ribs and
dishevel what was already unkempt,
fractured frames beneath the skin
that repeat interrogations
about how much a body
can curl into itself before breaking,
before being transformed entirely into
what is both haunted and terrible.

Avalanche

Omniscient fingers curl tight around
my throat where a cavern of tongues
detail every errant thought and an
avalanche of horror is swallowed quick.
My open mouth is grotesque and bare
in its frozen call for help. This is what it is
to no longer dream but to half-wake,
paralyzed by the monstrous shadows sewn
to my fingers, caught in a disaster of dark.
The escape is to wake, but I am betrayed.
My rented body, gaped in nightmare, pleads.
This is what it is to be denied in whole.
Choked, little jaws clench in defiance as
the renegade in the doorway advances,
unforgiving in its callous, wide embrace.

Some Things We Can't Speak About

this is me trying, satiated, though
a promise of settlement has been
whispered in my ear as we move,

and *does this make you happy?*
I ask with my tongue, hungry as
it continues to rain, a storm
that quiets only when you breathe,

but *haven't we been here before?*
when the rain is on its way down,
I sometimes think I can feel the earth
open, a wound, and it reminds me of
how it feels when you are in my mouth.

I Behold Your Brilliance And Have Found Home

People say they are puzzle pieces
made for one another.

But you and I, dearest:

You and I are the completed puzzle,
the whole picture, the entire design.
We were not placed together –
we simply became and we continue to be.

And then there's you, you alone.

You are the feathers of a starling,
light as you carry a body across this land
because flight is nothing but an adventure.

I watch your resolve and tremor in its wake.

You are the waves that refuse to drown the ocean,
a call to the waxing moon for a demanded response
in communication that swirls and meets the earth.

I absorb your strength and shiver in awe.

You are the wind and you speak through it
as though it had a name all along, one
you created and held on your determined tongue.

I behold your brilliance and have found home.

You are the riggings of the ship, our ship,
pushed and guided because you are also a compass
of a map to the treasure. And you, love, are the treasure.

You are, you are, you are.

Childhood

Barefoot, run across the asphalt as quick
as you can, child, for it is hot, so hot.
Bounce from one foot to the other, hop,
the floor is lava, child. Run through the grass,
feel its cool fingers tickle your toes, yes,
that's the stuff, of dirt and clay. Run –
across the sand, run towards the water, run
as though you are chased. Run, child, run.
The bottoms of your feet were made to be tough
because vulnerable is a word you have
not yet learned. Your feet were built for this,
child, darkened by the earth so that you could
become strong and willful in her image.
Carry forward. Your feet will become soft
with age as you forget all of this. You will
discover what it is to be vulnerable,
what it means to feel exposed, so you will
walk instead of run one day. But not this day,
child. Barefoot, run across the pavement, feel
the burn of the day linger on your skin again.
This will haunt you, child, this will fortify you:
remember how it feels to understand the
land because you've bared yourself for it,
a promise to return your body to its god.

Thoughts While Trying To Sleep

I can hear hands unclasp
in the night as the broken sigh
of prayers emerge like the whip-poor-wills,
sharp calls that say, *"I'm here, I'm here."*

I Know The Water Never Cared

after "Reading Hart Crane In Naples" by Ariel Francisco

In theory, I say, I am a bird - I
covet my hollow bones and know
I am delicate enough for air, the
words of others embody water
that slide off my feathers, but I never
believed it enough, you see, so I asked
for forgiveness when it was you
who brought it all down - this
question of falling or leaping - the
final deliverance has brought me to water
again, and so I float, float, never
to be bothered, despite who cared.

Devastated in Swaths of Color

Yarrows bloom from between my teeth,
and I swallow seeds meant to be planted.
I drink water and water and water until I am filled,
my skin soaked, though my eyes dry.
I can see others pretend I have not arrived,
my words buried beneath their muddy feet
as they run towards the life I am not meant to know.
But the sun casts shadows as much as it sheds light,
and I am understood, heard, seen within this land of birth.
I carve myself into bartered bark,
both devastated and deserved.
I see myself in the color green,
a signal of how I'm nascent and hopeful.
Soil is found beneath my nails in all the ways
I have touched experience. I am gathered in your hands,
a bouquet of trying. Pink and yellow and purple
rest on my tongue, and I smell the scent of familiarity.
Reciprocity spills itself upon your fingertips,
which I meet with my own. They touch my hair,
locks of revolution, and I smile - for I am spring.

This Is No Invocation

I fill my bedside glass,
wonder at its contents,
clear and cold.
This is no invocation.
I have nothing to proffer,
and my hands are obscene.
They shake in repose, mimic
the movement of faith.
The broken sigh of prayers
linger in a pause meant
to also be swallowed.
These prayers quench the
angry and starved and alone
from the ache of night.
As the tired begin to wake,
I can hear hands unclasp,
a quiet refrain of surrender.

Sedate Your Hesitation

after "A Certain Shade Of Green" by Incubus

I recall the summer when I started to spread my legs
as I discovered desire like I discovered music, a pinnacle time
of my teenage years soaked in premature alcoholism and
desperation for attention - *but what are you waiting for?* -
a certain shade of green, perhaps that of a hunter, flowered from between
my fingers and toes as I sank into the earth, prepared myself to bloom,
though I was made a woman before I knew how to wield that power.

I lost all words when I was buried... they fell from my head
and leaked from my ears and mouth, clung to my tongue as I tasted
loss and tried to take it back, swallow it whole, demand of myself
a strength I wasn't sure I had grown, grief a supple tree beginning
from a seed in my stomach, a dark room of strangers and ghosts
and outsiders that spoke a language I had not yet learned
- *but I am waiting.*

I mourned for who I was, the words I lost, the Denali mountain
I had to hike in order to see myself regain letters plucked
from the hills I traveled, separate the green fibers and feel them
with tired fingertips, divide the threads and run them up my arms
and around my neck, fists clenched with all I could hold, with
all I could stand. Choose now or lose it all.

Sorrow clung to my lungs as I struggled to breathe, and my body quaked
with the effort of not only burgeoning but also of waste, a
simultaneous design of a mountain turned over into itself, heaps of
grass and rock and weed devoured in the gulp of air taken as my body
shattered. This was the art, the act, the ruination as I became. I wait.
Yes, I'll wait and then I'll take flight, shades of green stitched to my feet.

Indicative of The Lost

I sit on the porch and listen to the chickadees,
so often named for their voice,
which always struck me as sweet,
eloquent destiny attached to their beaks.
I whisper, tempted by the notion.
The sun beats down on my thighs,
leaving a swift red birthmark across them,
a signature of kind. I am born in the daylight.
I straighten my arms overhead,
reach and stretch my body
like a piece of Juicy Fruit that clings to the tongue
and pushes its way from between these lips with a puff
to create the perfect bubble that pops at capacity,
of course it does, and then clutches the surface
of this mouth, that chin, this nose.
I pull the remnants from my face, a catastrophe of pink.
I press my sticky fingers into the burns of my legs,
watch as white dots bloom and fade
over and over again. I think to myself,
surely, there is more here to remember.

There Is No Such Thing As Nothing

There is no such thing as nothing: not in this body.

The center of my abdomen and the curve of my ankles
and the notches of bone in my neck and every little knuckle.

The focus of the universe is found
behind the treeline veins of my eyes
but also in the bullfrog outside my window

and also in the pink of your palms and
also in the hungry summer heat.
You smile and say you love it here.

My temperament understands more now
that the past is no longer accosted by it.

There is no such thing as nothing: not in this world.

I spell beauty on your lips and can taste myself,
and this is how I know. The rearrangement of these words
rearranges the universe, and I am but one – centered.

Gaping, Girl

We hiked in the dead of summer, dead on our feet, dead ahead.
We stroked between our breasts and swiped at the sweat pooled there,
this most sensitive spot. Climb, girl. We are not fooled, girl. A cavern
in your mouth, gaping, girl. Seek the forsaken and kiss their graves;
turn them, I'm sure, with sticky lips and porous teeth. We are only
meant to dive off a cliff for the mourners. We hear our body speak, girl.
By September you'll have sewn your skin back into place and smiled
in response to the ones who have found safety, kissed their fiends,
dissolved despite, despite. We reach the top this time, forsaken the
monsters to the abandoned, and breathe, girl, while deciding what
to do with this new knowledge, a woman now, who tastes herself.

&

In the gold of the ampersand,
a note finds its way
from your hand to mine
 - symphony.
An upheaval of red
as your tongue
slides in my mouth.
Pardon me.
The sparrows have more to say
now than ever
as their little beaks emerge
 - open, frail - and yet.
Unable to change a thing.
Our eyes find their bodies.
What benefits us?
In the amber, cicadas
mate and then die,
a moment everyone
must think about
- at least once.
I'm sorry.
We just want to be
found, a conjunction
that pieces this together.
And becomes then.

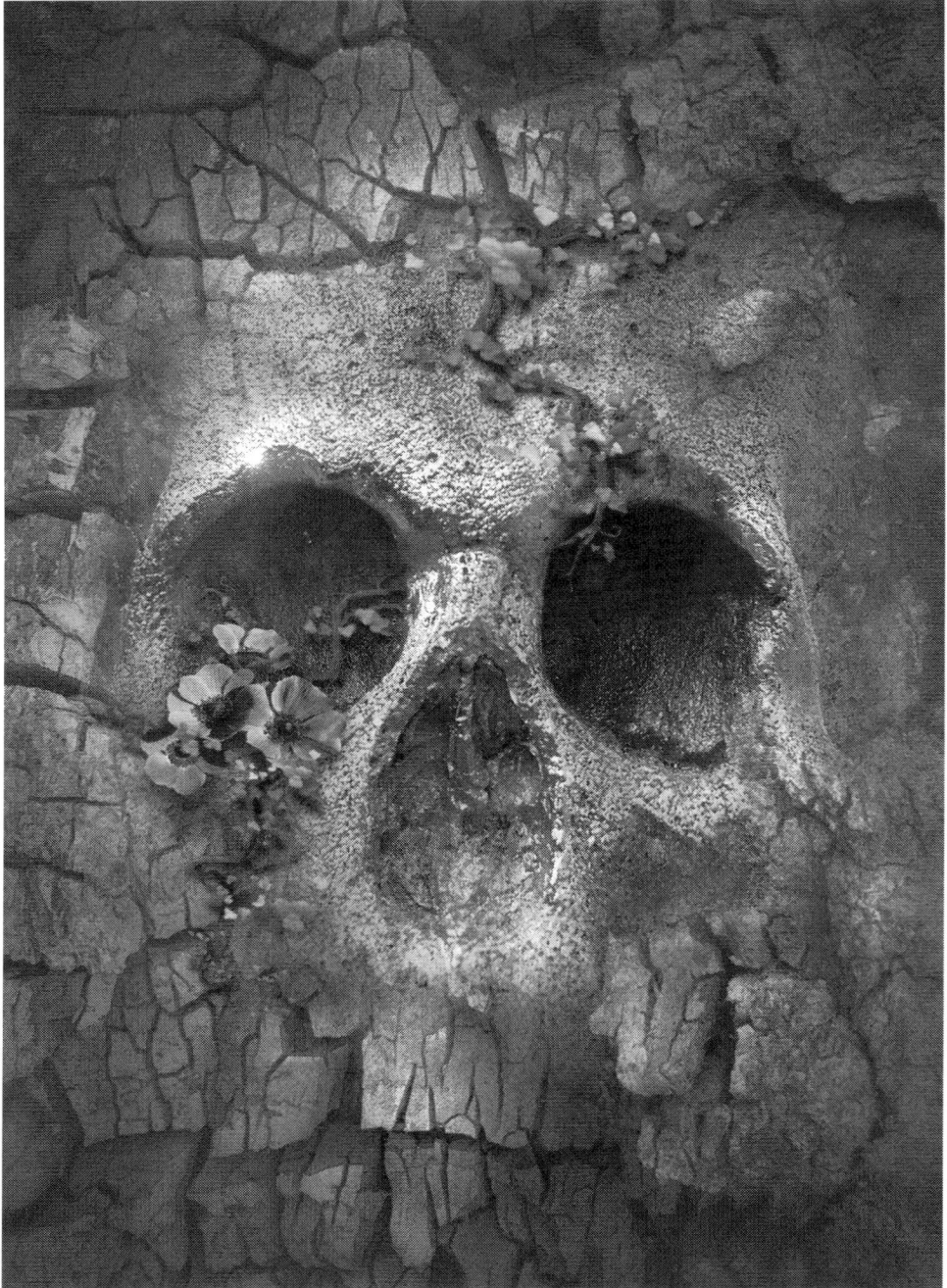

Acknowledgements

Writing may be a solo endeavor, but no writer is ever truly alone. The inspiration comes from a multitude of places, but most importantly, it comes – at least for me – from my loved ones.

I must thank my dear friend and eternal confidant, Brandon, for allowing me to run my dreaded first drafts by you. You always manage to offer such imperative insight and have no doubt made me a better writer, a better friend, a better person. I am grateful for everything. Everything.

My sister, Cassandra, of course, along with Jonathon, Lukas, and Caden, have all been so supportive of me along the way. I am in continued awe by your kindness and resilience, dear "seester," and I am always buoyed by your encouragement.

I want to also thank my friend, René, for being one of the first to read *Chiseled Teeth*. Your intuition and aptitude as both a bibliophile and a writer are unparalleled and therefore are an amazing gift to this chapbook and to me.

I have an amazing therapist to thank, for her discernment and understanding of the way my brain works has helped me become a better version of myself and therefore better able to create *Chiseled Teeth*.

To everyone who has ever bought a commissioned poem from me, thank you so much for trusting me to create a product worthy of you. Those commissions gave me a newfound light in the sometimes creative darkness and doubt, and they offered me a chance to stretch outside my comfort zone. Some of those pieces made it into this collection, and they obviously would not exist without you.

It is in moments like these that words do not feel like enough. I hope this collection speaks to how much you all mean to me, how much I adore each and every one of you, and how much of myself belongs to you. Thank you for not only joining me on this journey but for helping me get here.

(The following poems were published prior to inclusion in this chapbook: "Don't Pick The Flowers" in Emerge Literary Journal, "Peak, South Carolina" in All Female Menu, "This Is No Invocation" in Variant Literature, and "&" in Beyond Words Magazine.)

Ashley Logan

Ashley Logan (she/her) resides in Columbia, South Carolina, with her anxious but loyal dog, Barkley.

She earned a Bachelor of Arts degree in English from the University of South Carolina in 2010 and has been published in various magazines over the years.

When not writing, she enjoys traveling, buying too many books and even reading some of them, as well as dabbling in photography.

She can be found on Twitter (@loganashes) and Instagram (@logan.ashes).

Made in the USA
Las Vegas, NV
07 April 2022